Eternal Life in Time
(2019)

*

essay

*

Traumear

*

We may be familiar with the concept 'eternal life' and we may wonder how such life compares with our daily existence from time to time. We may also be familiar with the Christian notion of eternal life and with the various supernatural and other-worldly ideas in connection with it. In this little essay I make a comparison with human development and evolution to show how eternal life here and now, in time, is what we enjoy once we have developed to the point of evolution; in other words once we are sufficiently mature to cooperate in the process of our resurrection.

*

Eternal Life in Time

It would seem reasonable to suppose that in order for us to be able to live eternally and to perceive that we do so, we would have to be in time, otherwise our contact with our senses would deteriorate. Once we feel certain that eternal life is on the cards for us we will not rest until we have personal experience of it. We will not be content with assurances of its existence at some date in the future. As a consequence we tend to alter our approach to the sensible world and to our inward being until we can make some sense of the life that is eternal here and now.

We cannot live eternally and in time at the same time, that stands to reason, so when we say that we have eternal life in time we must mean that we *are* in time, while we live eternally. The difference between being and living does therefore need to be looked at. From our present point of view only one possibility exists for us to do this. We look for it the creative domain, at the point of growth.

*

Perhaps we pay too little attention to being, to what we do when we are. Indeed, doing and being cannot be imagined simultaneously, which may account for that lack of discrimination that can only be ascertained in terms of thought. So we suppose that we either are or we do. Does that mean that we either are or we live? It would be a great pity if we were only playing with words. Imagination will serve us well either on the side of being or during the process of doing and living but it will not bridge the gap between the two. I wonder why that is. There must be some good reason for it. I imagine it has to do with our deplorable habit of imagining indistinctly. We do not allow images to become real while we imagine and as a result it happens that they carry us away into an unreal world – where we then crave reality and hunger for it. Oh when will our saviour come! We even work ourselves up into diverse ecstasies upon which we then dwell in these artificially hopeful states while we tell ourselves that we have 'at least that' in the meantime, while we 'faithfully and patiently wait'.

What, is it all a matter of imagining indistinctly?

I fear that it may be. As for that being all – well, centuries pass and each generation teaches the next to imagine indistinctly. Wars are fought to drive home truths based on indistinct imagination. We wish it were otherwise.

*

Let us for a moment consider what it means to be; not even to be around, but merely to be. We can do that, it's no trouble. We switch off all our various mental and bodily mechanisms – they only get us into trouble in any case – and we allow ourselves to drift upon the moment. Time passes and we take no issue with that. Let time pass, we refuse to quarrel with it. We simply are and we know it.

Should we imagine the passage of time as a stream of sweet water between banks of fragrant bougainvillea? Actually I believe bougainvillea are not even fragrant but no matter, we can imagine as we please. We can believe as we please too. We believe that time is passing like an imagined stream of sweet water between banks of fragrant pink and white bougainvillea. – I apologize to the reader; what I have been imagining all along is not bougainvillea but oleander and no wonder, because only yesterday I returned from Crete where the main national road is often lined with huge red or white oleander shrubs. I can actually picture various sections of that road now, on the way from Aghios Nikolaos to Chania, beautifully lined on both sides at times by this poisonous shrub – someone told me that one-hundred grams of the sweet leaves is enough to kill a horse.

Now we turn off our imagination and our picturing faculty again and return to being as such. Why would anyone do that, when it's so much more entertaining to imagine and to picture? Well, our only reason for doing it just now is to emphasize the difference between being and living. Usually we like to differentiate between being and doing, however there is no clear-cut difference in reality, as we noticed just now when being invited us, almost against our will, to imagine and to picture. As soon as we returned to 'mere' being we felt quite bereft, rather imprisoned within ourselves, as though we were trying to be just a little perverse. So it seems that being as such, or mere being, may well be possible, at least for a while, but it may not be advisable. Of course when we do, we also are, surely that goes without saying, but when we are without doing we are to some extent violating our nature which, as we surely all agree, is not a good thing to do. I dare say we 'fall into it' if we are not sufficiently careful. Then what can happen, if we have drifted in unimagined being for a time, like a thing lost to the world, is that we are disgusted with ourselves and we look for a way out of our self-imposed dead end. We cannot think properly, so we reach for some hallucinogenic substance to fool our bereft system – or rather ourselves – into a state of what we might call psychic imagination, which is nothing real but a poor substitute. Psychic systems and states can become chronic, as we know all too well. They are externally produced internal states. I feel inclined to call them falsehoods, or just plain lies. They are wanderings of the mind in the Land of Nod and a poor substitute for human being. Also there is no direct route from such states in the direction of human being. In other words we cannot, in hallucinogenic terms, define human reality, so the only way out of this falsehood is by concentration upon the truth and by desire for truth.

While we are on the subject, we may as well remind ourselves that mere being, as the accident that it is, can be prevented. We can behave in a way that makes accidents of mere being most unlikely. However before we go into that, I would like to look at the other side of the false coin, when we are not dealing with internal or psychic states, externally produced, but with external or ecstatic states, internally produced. This is again something that happens, that is accidental, but now, in our state of mere being, we are so eager that we should possess real signs for the actual existence of something we fervently desire or hope for, that internally we produce ecstasies that belie externally what cannot exist outwardly.

Both hallucinations and ecstasies are consequences due to combinations of mere being and indistinct imagination. Both internally produced external abnormalities and externally induced internal abnormalities, which is to say ecstasies and hallucinations, are nonetheless evidence of dissatisfaction with mere being and of attempts to secure amelioration by means of indistinct imagination.

*

We might ask how mere being comes about in the first place. It would not occur to a mature human being to entertain it. This is because maturity implies growth and the will or desire to grow, so that anything that impedes or undermines mature growth is rejected out of hand. However, as we know fine well by now in our twenty-first century, human maturity is no function of the technical will and intellect. If our efforts at increase and fruition remain uninformed by good spirit, we move in circles and leave ourselves open to external and internal persuasions. Mere being does in fact imply this openness to internal and external affectation, so that all too readily we turn away from outward and inward influence.

The more I think about it, the more do I realize that mere being can turn into an attractive option for those who feel themselves destined for some high office, for some especial favour that they suppose will come their way if they allow themselves to turn into an object or into a subject. I think that this is what we have to look at if we wish to understand the various phenomena that accrue in the wake of mere being, when the very suggestion of inward and outward reality is anathema. It is that this reality is not one-sided, not worth bleeding for and never existential in isolation – such as an object and a subject. Those who speak of objective reality have something in mind that matches their subjective existence – and vice versa. Yes, here we have stumbled upon the secret of mere being as an actual choice. Right up to this point, when one still toys with the notion of having a choice, even while allowing oneself to drift with the very possibility of non-being, the other possibility exists also, namely the one that is usually called: asking for help. We drift but we suppose there is still time, if worse comes to worst, to return to the state prior to when we began to drift.

Then we choose objectivity or subjectivity for our normality and begin to behave in any of the great number of possible ways that will allow us to justify our choice. Or put it this way: we behave so as to justify our choice. It is bound to seem very much in our interest that we avoid impartial reality, however we will only succeed in this to the degree that we manage to insist on either objective or subjective survival.

This is where survival comes into its own. Survival, in comparison to life, is objective or subjective. We do not necessarily hallucinate or become ecstatic, but all too often it seems we cannot help ourselves, and then we feel it must be up to us to be able to vouch for these extreme phenomena, so we defend them and ourselves in terms of them. We are liable to base our beliefs on them, to swear by them in a court of law and to accuse one another of infidelity in relation to them.

It goes without saying that the hallucinations of one generation are the festivals of the next and the ecstasies of one culture bear no resemblance to those of another. Extreme phenomena, however, are never significant; the objective or subjective states in which they originate do however bear a kind of significance, so that those who know and understand outward and inward reality may identify them.

*

5

Our reason for identifying objective or subjective phenomena, always as laws or states, is that we may allow them to come true. In themselves they are of no interest to us. Whatever grows organically shuns mere being in the interest of live being. Live beings do however, as it were, rub up against mere beings – which results in a kind of two-way traffic. Remember that mere beings cannot be studied as such because they exist in a state of flux. Nonetheless our live being initially reacts to objective and subjective phenomena, to states and laws that are incomplete in themselves, because of the magical terrain that is produced by them, the aura that suggest the possibility of perfect order and total control. An excitement wells up in us that draws immediate attention to itself and invites us to participate in these magical pursuits that promise a world of permanence and finality over which we shall rule.

Magic and sorcery, to be fair, do present themselves as sober pursuits of knowledge and understanding, however always under the aegis of the supreme survival tactic – I mean the one that promises to make it possible for us to reject eternal life by surviving forever. Something like eternal survival is pictured and pursued and the strategies that are imagined as media of success in that direction are presented enthusiastically in public, both objectively and subjectively, as science and art.

The significance of this science and art, for live beings now, is twofold. By not rejecting it, as we may feel like doing, we become capable of the high tolerance that we need in any case if we are to extend our sphere of influence in line with the generous spirit that supports us in our pursuit of reality – and by not judging it, as we do suppose we should, at times, in the interest of true knowledge and understanding, we develop the sense of fairness and equanimity that is required if we are ever to learn how to judge righteously and mercifully.

Notice that we make headway, for ourselves, in the proximity of mere being, not so much by what we do but rather by what we refrain from doing. This is interesting in itself. We refrain from judging that which is even then in the process of being judged and we do not reject that which is being rejected even as we perceive it. Little by little we develop the supreme insight that is required of us so that we may exemplify live being. High tolerance and merciful judgement become second nature to us.

*

We are not to interfere with that which is being rejected and judged. We are not to reject mere beings nor are we to judge them. This may be a difficult lesson to learn for those who are overly enthusiastic in their work or they make the mistake of hoping to be able to correct themselves by correcting others. Let them be reminded that the process of judgment and rejection continues also in live beings. Our resurrection is not simply a process of steady absorption of new life. What about the old life that has to make way for it? Of course we are wise to concentrate on the new life while we let the judgment and rejection within us take care of itself. So must we let the judgment and rejection take care of itself in others, even and especially in those who have no new life, lest we become entangled in their diverse problematic states, which would be no use at all to them and a digression for us.

Those who are never done looking for original causes may surely be permitted to imagine that human beings are created perfect and sent out to take on the imperfection of all creation. Their ability to arrive at this final understanding, which is what they have always longer for, implies now that they joyfully take on the task of helping to raise all creation to that final evolutionary level from where no improvement may be envisioned. I see no reason why this should not be a perfectly legitimate way of approaching – and embracing – that final goal of humanity. Those to whom it is not given to cooperate in the resurrection work have their destiny cut out for them and while

7

we can see the rejection and judgment at work in them, they themselves, as we can see all around us, do not seem particularly upset by their state of mere being. They do what they do as always. While they are not allowed to interfere with us, neither does it make any sense that we should interfere with them.

*

What I want to come around to now is time itself and to the way that it may either be perceived or not. Please keep in mind what we have learned in terms of live being and mere being.

Time perceived is always an enrichment. Even those who avoid time-perception are now and again blessed with that momentary insight into how we would be if time were not. It is not an insight that increases our wisdom but it allows us to appreciate the time it takes to do what we do more successfully.

Without time we would wither and die. It would take no time at all. The absurdity of trying to imagine a timeless state has to be brought home to us now and again if we become too much diverted by those ideal processes and idealistic states that some of the religions of the world dangle in front of us as the reward for sitting in their pews. A timeless state of being, to come right out with it, is a non-sequitur. Which is not to say that an overwrought soul will not reach for psychic defence mechanisms to remind us of our lack of grip on reality. However here too the historic process, for all it is worth, has seen fit to embed in the popular tradition all those diverse dogmas and beliefs that confuse the sign with that of which it is a sign. The psychic defence mechanisms are signs of an overwrought soul, not precious indications of future blessedness to which we may attain. A medicinal draught relieves us of emergent pain. Will we now continue to imbibe that draught? Surely not.

There are states of time, impressions of time and long-winded appropriations of time, all available on the modern marketplace and we wish those the best of luck who choose to entertain themselves in terms of them. What matters to us is that we

8

know the gift for the gracious generosity of the giver. Are we not on the lookout for every possible move we might make to establish ourselves more securely in the tripartite position of collaborators, corroborators and co-operators with that glorious spirit that seeks to conjoin with us, his chosen creation, in life on earth at the centre of the universe?

I suppose there might be more acceptable ways to persuade the sceptical modernist of the point I wish to make. However we ourselves feel approached from a thousand different directions by that spirit, so we too need to branch out, as we realize that, as always, the same word means many things for many; it must be context that carries the gist of our meaning, and context diversifies and concentrates like the universe itself.

*

We like to be punctual, on time, however being 'in' time is something else. How, for example, can we be in time if we do not grow? Live beings make growth their existential habit. They do not shrug off the responsibility of being around for one another, for several and for many and they understand what is in it for them. No need for morality to persuade them to do what is good for them, namely, for but one example, community in time. I tend to feel rather partial to this concept of community in time. It helps to keep me grounded. For that same reason I get annoyed when I have to struggle to make myself understood for no other reason than that the modern ear is unwilling to hear. It attaches itself to some distant star rather than one on each side of a human head.

Here and now I would like to develop in greater detail what I mean by community in time. We have two ears and two eyes, even two nostrils and so on, so we like to take hold of what we suspect might do us a bit of good on both sides, with the compact substance of it safe in the middle. So in that sense and with that particular intention firmly in place, we inspect communal time as both dynamic and static, as both motive and inert, as both

9

traditional and new. Historically there is so much to be said about our forefathers' stated preferences that we may safely pick and choose as we see fit and no need to fear the Philistine. Cult, tribe and nation, as complexes of meaning, do, in spite of our love of argument, contain that unmistakable kernel of elementary reality that allow us, honourably, to draw conclusions from them in the ontological direction of community, even if, by community, we only mean a verbal bond and an essential point of agreement. At the same time we know that a tribe must needs define itself against another tribe, a nation against another nation, while cults have the hardest time in the world, usually, to define themselves without stepping on a great number of unsuspecting toes.

The verbal bond, in comparison now to all else that might persuade us to sing from the same hymn sheet, depends solely upon the truthful word with real meaning. The essential point of agreement – if we wish to approach from that other direction – depends on love and good will.

If we consider 'being in time' as essential and concrete – why would we ever not be in time? Is it not because time informs us of our mortality and we do not always wish to be reminded? Whyever not, I wonder! If we were not liable to die, how would we be free to choose life? So are we up against a simple case of misunderstanding? We are liable to die and at the same time we may choose life. Does not very choice imply the possibility of no choice? The truthful word with real meaning is not an accident or even a categoric imperative but a human achievement in cooperation with merciful good spirit. Similarly love and good will can be utterly avoided by us, even intentionally if we put our minds to it. If we choose to love and to exercise good will, are we not at the same time aware of how readily this intention is prone to confusion and how it needs to be renewed every day, refurbished perhaps several times during the day – if indeed we wish to grow and to mature? Surely the work we choose to do aids and abets our growth, so that we will not repeatedly or even continually be in need to be corrected, to be reminded, to be punished, judged and set straight?

Ah, now this brings nicely into line our choice of work and our perception of time. I think we might just gaze for a moment in the direction of our goal, to behold how it appears to us. Can we behave in a way that will assure for us that we stay in time? Of course patience comes to mind. Our intact soul, remember, desires to remain in our possession, if I may put it like that and I don't see why I shouldn't. So much depends on whether we remain in the possession of our soul so that it will not need to shout for help. Mere being does without a soul but this does not concern us here. Our essay is transporting us in the direction of live being, eventually culminating in eternal life.

*

Our work is always at least creative, in that it overcomes the allures of mere being and the temptations of useless rejection and judgment. So if part of our work is to remain in time – and, by the way, to return into time if ever we have strayed – then we have to be aware of something in time that will either further our ends or be an end in itself. The ends of the earth, for example, are all timely. Earth as our habitat! Oh how it melts my heart once again to be brought home to the notion of earth as our habitat! To be brought home in time. Some are born and among us that have never been away and we can learn much from them – mostly how to be in time graciously. "This one thing I will do for the rest of my life now," says the Mongolian peasant who is determined to save the native honeybee from extinction. One seems to hear the intention to prevail in time while nurturing one of the ends of the earth. And who was it that promised to be with us even to the ends of the earth? Remind me. Enough said, we are never alone while we are in time.

So are we to be in time so as not to be alone? Remember we have a choice. There is that which draws us out of time. I call it the curse of predestination. Not the blessing but the curse of it. It's a blessing to know where we are meant to go if we know who does the meaning and that the meaning is merciful good spirit. It's a curse to suppose you are destined to die in time. Naturally, in that case, you would want to escape from time. Not human-naturally but naturally. Because time is imagined as the enemy. Time as death. That must be awful. The gift intended as a blessing turns out to be a poisoned apple.

Consider, however, who is responsible for that curse. Ask anyone who rushes through the day as fast as he can and at night he does battle with insomnia who it was, who is to blame, for representing time as the curse. He will hate you for asking him a stupid question. Why should he bother taking the time to answer such a stupid question? Modern man is to be pitied because he is in such a hurry to go nowhere. If only something were to stop him in his tracks! If only that were enough to allow him to come to his senses!

Precious time! Actually we have more time than a whale in the ocean has water.

What, however, are we supposed to do with all this time? Well, to be sure, it's not there for us to do anything with. It's not there at all. That is a common mistake to make, to suppose that time is there. "You are wasting time, dear. And you are wasting my time. Time is money." Well, there you have it. Need one say more? Time is money. Is that what you believe? Well, now and again, I suppose.

The earth takes time and time reveals the earth to us. Try that on for size. Why should the earth be of interest? Why should the house we live in be of interest? When the roof leaks, when the thatch catches fire – is that interesting? Or maybe you live in a shack full of litter, what do I know. The northern provinces of China are being swept away by sand. There's no need for that. In my town here the footpaths are being resurfaced ever so carefully. I'm not saying that a lot of people take notice but order and hygiene have a subtle effect. So let's take the time to look at the earth and soon that will occur to us as a most appropriate type of behaviour. Take the time to look at the earth and see what you can see. It's a start. So much time suddenly rises to the surface because you are willing to make good use of it. How much longer will the demons be allowed to ravage our homesteads? Only until we take the time to look and see what is going on; what is being done and what is not being done.

*

I suggested to a young man he might do what he was doing in good spirit. He blanched, his eyes searched for the enemy and he said: "There's no need to bring religion into it."

Is it any wonder? Look what is being perpetrated – what has so often in the past been perpetrated in the name of religion. Let's not go into it. However good spirit we cannot do without if we want to be in time on earth. Good spirit is what causes the earth to thrive and to offer up its wealth. I mention good spirit as a sort of basket concept now, because I don't want to get involved in any religion. If you want to be in time on earth you have to be motivated by good spirit, otherwise things go awry. Look for good spirit within yourself. It wells up as soon as you look for it. It wells up as motivation. Good motivation. Off you go now, do some good.

Please take notice, we are still in time on earth while we allow ourselves to be motivated by good spirit. Now here is a thought that will cheer you: The same good spirit that wells up within you whenever you ask for it to motivate you to do good also shapes the earth in its splendour and munificence. And here is a thought that may surprise you: That same good spirit cannot shape the earth unless it has your cooperation. This allows you to think of good spirit as preternaturally human. Go on from there and think of humanity as the essence of all being and you are well on your way to behave ethically. You will do good in cooperation with good spirit. You will know that your cooperation is necessary in both directions – to define yourself as a human being and to have an effect in time on earth that helps to shape the earth. Is the earth not in shape? Well, believe me, it could do with a little help. It hangs over the edge of the balcony four stories up. It needs to trim its nails but has no one to hold the light up close. Gases escape from it that testify to a moribund digestion. At the same time it's out there pitching. These days we need to realize how we've just allowed ourselves to abuse the earth, ignorantly, as though it were a dead rock, and we kick it out of our way. Well, some of us do, not everybody. A lot of good work is being done. We need to pay attention, because so much is happening so fast these days and when people get into a panic they get busy in the wrong way. They tackle the fire by throwing dry wood on it.

Ignore good spirit within you and be part of the problem. What is the problem – worth probing? Ignorance of the fact that man is responsible for the earth. Refusal to countenance how human beings, earth and good spirit are bonded.

*

Consider this for a definition: Earth is material in flux. Heraclitus had his finger on it when he suggested that 'panta rhei'; it all flows. Then we need to add our ability to instigate good change. It flows this way and that way and it waits patiently for us to steer it. Participate in the flow by all means but realize that it's not good flow until you cooperate with good spirit. The work you do makes all the difference, good or bad. Do good work. Cooperate with good spirit. Stay on earth in time and do good work in cooperation with good spirit. The deserts will bloom again. The black rhino will recover. And if the glaciers melt, that is not necessarily a bad thing. Calm down. Don't pretend to know everything, in your post-modern scientific fervour. Number-crunching will not mend your soul. What soul, you say? Exactly!

*

14

Our attitude to earth-existence gradually changes these days. We are turning into care-takers. We take pride in the fact, in the privilege, that we exist on earth. This has been the one single fact of what is loosely called space-conquest, that we learn to appreciate more fully that which fills our space, namely earth. It's why we go on holiday to Formica. We appreciate our home again, perhaps to a higher level. Familiarity breeds contempt. Mind you, after a while we will have visited all the possible Formicas and then we will learn to turn upon the enemy contempt directly. We will check out what exactly we mean by familiarity. Suddenly judgement is upon us and we welcome it. Crunch time is not something to escape from but something to participate in. Let's not try to escape from time this time but let's instead look it in the face, get a feel for it, welcome it to the family dinner table. Mind you, this can be overdone. Then lethargy sets in. A weird sluggishness that makes us suppose we would best stay in bed until some emergency drags us out of it. It is the indolence of timelessness. Look at your watch. Do you realize it's lunchtime? What have you been doing? Nothing? For six hours? I've been up and about, feeding the chickens, scrubbing the tiles, dusting the piano and writing a letter of condolence to aunt Madge in the care home.

I'm sorry, I just don't care. My survival is not at risk, and as a direct consequence I disintegrate. I let the wind blow past my cheeks and listen to the thumping of my heart in my chest. Secretly I am persuaded that time is not actually something we can realistically or hopefully escape from. At present, you see, I experiment with time. There is purpose to my apparent lassitude. I don't mind if for the moment you are upset with me, Martha. I am the Mary who, for the moment, chooses the better part. I am waiting patiently for time to reveal to me its inmost secret. I am willing to wait for a lifetime, that is the only way I will achieve my goal. So I have my eyes open, this is true, I am not nodding off, but my brain is in neutral. I have stopped at the red light, foot on the clutch, other foot on the break, out of gear, watching those two elderly ladies on the pedestrian crossing. They take their time as I take mine. There seems to be plenty for all of us. I think to myself: 'What is the secret of time?' Such a bottomless pit over which I may hover, gravity disengaged, the motor still running. Can it even be put into words, this secret? I will not get the hang of it if I ignore the red light and forget that eventually I will move off, home – to make lunch for the family, check those statements from the bank, sort those boxes in the attic. The secret of time is – its sheer endlessness. I have it now. And suddenly my hand cramps so that I can barely continue to type this sentence. Time is endless but not to be endlessly indulged. There comes a time when it wants to be invested – put it that way. Red changes to yellow, then green. I have learned something and I have passed it on to you. The endlessness of time. No such thing as the end of time.

So what is the implication? Take your time but get cracking. If time is not invested it bites the hand that feeds it. Laziness, tiredness, weariness set in and we contemplate moribundity, as if that were a word. We act as if we had never heard of action. We behave stupidly. We become 'thick'.

And this is only the other side of how we misbehave when we hurry and haste and then waste. Fast is how everything has to be done. Not quickly but fast. The faster the better because you can get more time. Try to run the fastest mile in the world. See how many strawberries you can pick in one hour and still straighten up with your back killing you. Don't wait for the wife to finish her endless sentences but rush off, you have things to do, buttons to push, money to make, minds to change. Expedite the unwillingness of your popular environment. The time is limited. It is allotted in coffee spoons to the deserving. Best of all, invent machines to speed up the process so that you can sit back and watch. Then invent a faster machine. Learn to type faster. With a bit of luck you will never again make a mistake. Computers swallow time by the bucket-load until none is left. – Hold on, how is that possible? I thought time was endless. Ah, but you see, the time that is swallowed by machines is not the real thing but a simulacrum. "Malvolio, hie thee!" cries Olivia and sends him to perform his pointless chore. He performs it unwillingly. He rightly feels put upon. He shall have his revenge on the lot of them.

*

Why is it so difficult to imagine time? Because we have to imagine in time. Imagination bypasses whatever in its essence is timeless and depicts it in some lasting fashion. This annoys those among us who would much prefer to sit idly while they let the world spin on their fingers. So externally, time makes sense as clock-time. There we can imagine it as whatever takes seconds, minutes and hours. The calendar is a help. Internally, by comparison, time is patience or haste. We feel time slipping by and know that a watched kettle won't boil. The very anxiety of our modern soul is a result of our trying to imagine time internally. Why can we not trust the seasons? If we did, I mean completely trust them, there would be no more need to meddle with our soul in terms of psychic phenomena and stop clocks. The seasons inspire us with time – if we let them – that is neither external nor internal but eternal. Eternal time is much closer to us than our watch or our feelings – which is precisely why we shun it or shrug it off. We are committed to living our lives either externally or internally because that is how life addresses us. One moment we have to catch a train and the next moment we dread the consequences of being late for work. We are as it were strung out on this polarity and this is not due to anything we have done. It's how it is. Don't we at least have to accept reality as it is? Our scientists teach us to take pride in that. Meanwhile they dig more and more deeply and presumably with greater thoroughness and authority into the outside and the inside reality. Their disciplines, as they call them, allow them to concentrate on one or the other. They are specialists in reality-halves even as they present their findings as milestones along the road to true reality in the end.

No need to exaggerate. Eternal understanding however makes it its task to conjoin the external with internal and to withhold its pronouncements until they refer to the whole. A true science would therefore have to begin with the scientist – who obviously would not call himself that now – conjoining the two halves of the modern consciousness within himself. Suddenly he would be able to speak – would be justified in speaking – of reality within. That would have to be his start before he presumed to be able to look at the world through unbiased senses.

Why would he not call himself a scientist? Because he is no longer an individual. Nor an individualist. He no longer parades his individuality in public, with the aim of drawing attention to himself and to his findings, but he realizes that the life we find is not worth the paper it is printed on and as a consequence he hides his individuality and allows it to get to work.

The scientist, as a modern individual, more or less consciously interferes with reality and then studies the effects of his interference. As an individual he is one-sided, so of course his effects must be one-sided. What he ends up with is always half the story. This can be immensely interesting to us as modern individuals and as we know, it is productive of 'great wonders' – that either take us in or wear us out. They confirm us in our modernity. They take us further and further away from our true reality, I am sorry to say. Most impressive, all the same. Soon we will be able to circumnavigate the globe in half an hour while we comprehend our psyche as a complex of an infinite number of syndromes – but will we be able to get on with our wives? I don't think so. As soon as the sex or the electricity is turned off we are in the dark in more ways than one.

No need to exaggerate. It will all come right in the end. Impossible to ignore the life within forever. The life within –

which develops and then evolves as eternal life – is eventually irresistible. It persuades by being. A very little suffices to begin with. Then it makes inroads. We withdraw from the modern half-life for a while. Our human nature draws attention to itself. The nature of the scientist is no longer all that interesting; I mean the nature the scientist finds interesting – the nature that is objective or subjective but never both. The nature that enters upon our corpus delicti as data and statistical information and leaves it as a swarm of bees.

*

Eternal time is a concept beyond which we cannot think rationally. It becomes necessary to locate within ourselves the source of those limitations and disciplines that allow us to behave creatively, which is to say within sight and awareness of ourselves as dual, not whole. I know there are some who would benefit from knowing that in our duality we are actually better off than when we were still at the mercy of demons without knowing it. Our limitations in those days were set by forces beyond our ken and control and when we acted we automatically played into the hands of death, however we imagined it. All we can say about that time is that it was prior to the time when 'left was divided from right', when reality was no longer allowed to be massive and when more and more human beings became capable of discerning spirits. By this I mean that they could tell the difference between the two sides that were coming into view and it was given to them that they should be able, in their own way, to join those two sides up. To marry them, as it were. One example of this could be sited as a becoming *conscious* of reality as objective or subjective and a becoming *aware* of the possibility of resurrection. By resurrection would right away have been meant the reestablishment of world as one 'even as at the beginning'. Initial expressions of this were bound to remain mythic and metaphoric. Nonetheless there have been isolated cases for two-thousand years of the cosmic life coming into view, always personal and unique. The false incorporation of that life in a nation and as national could only take hold for a time, even like the eruptions of pious mysticism, which, like nationalism, could be described as the hurried and lazy attempt to deal with the new reality. Urgency was turned – or was allowed to turn – into emergency. Many attempts were made to integrate eternal time in terms of clock time – that would be one way of putting it. Meanwhile life lived in eternal time surfaced sporadically. What was missing was an example of such time lived in total reliance on truth. The resurrected personality had not until then become established on earth. Now it's in the wind and the climate changes.

*

As a result of eternal time becoming 'feasible', shall we say, the human personality was perceived as the true 'outpouring', as it were, of human nature. In other words, human nature and personality were practically reinvented to fit in with eternal life experience – even though eternal life experience itself was more instinctive than reasonable.

I am trying to come to terms here with that point of departure from the ghostly reality that refuses to remain either visible or invisible, to the reality in which one worships and which itself, in the meanwhile, becomes more and more desirable. I maintain that there is good reason for coming to terms with it, I mean rather than right away presuming to depict the final reality as achievement. It is after all the turning point for many, at a time when they either trust themselves into the arms of the 'I am that I am', after years of dithering in the throes of what they are practically forced, by their many appetites, to reject time and again as just plain insufficient, threadbare; lacking in substance – or else they sink back/rush off into drugged states. When it dawns on them that the identification of a supposed lack of substance may also be understood as a conceivable presence or availability of substance, what they need is a little encouragement to take that last step – which I at the moment am trying to describe. It is substance as inherent rather than as imagined that we are all looking for – we who can no longer bear to think of a finality of world without accusing ourselves of not trying hard enough. At that precise moment, what we might welcome most is the assurance that substance itself is just then eager to reveal itself to us. I am put in mind of Michelangelo's great masterpiece painted on the Sistine Chapel ceiling – which I have always understood as the resurrection of the new Adam. God and man reach out to each other.

The purpose of trying to depict this point of departure is therefore foremost in my mind. The 'I am that I am' reaches out to those who make the least bit of effort to do a bit of reaching out themselves. At the same time there is no getting through to those who have drugged themselves by insisting on one side of the modern dichotomy or by indulging themselves in the other.

*

The imagined life is called survival. We survive by avoiding danger or by courting danger. We survive by not eating too much and not eating too little – in other words by concentrating on the mean between two opposites. Be careful, don't overdo it. Take care of yourself. Look after yourself. Be self-sufficient. Pull your weight in society so that you don't become a burden on the State. 'Get a life!' means get out of my hair and find something interesting to do. Keep busy. Concentrate on you health too. Health is all-important. It's obvious. When you are sick you become a burden for others. Why? Because they feel obliged to make you live as long as possible. Of course one can imagine a society where anyone who shows the least signs of some malaise is immediately incinerated. The mere sight of him makes others uneasy – and hateful. Needless to say there would be a lot of pretending then. I'm not sick, honestly, I just momentarily allowed the corners of my mouth to go down. – Don't let it happen again.

Mind you, some of that pretending goes on in any case, on account of the survival instinct. The barbarian, who is trying to avoid modernity, throws himself to the left or the right and never looks back. The survival instinct is his raison d'être and he swears by it, loudly. I don't believe that the pious socialist ever dares to confront him. The barbarian has no qualms about using force to gain his ends. Evil is a stupid mistake and good is what you can get away with. Self-interest is holy. He smiles when some modern religionist comes to his door with leaflets. Poor sucker. Also the barbarian might be a billionaire or a car salesman, let's not get *that* wrong. He might even have made his pile out of inventing a religion. The god of survival throws money around him like confetti. Or he just plain enjoys the cut and thrust of salesmanship.

Mind you again, it takes a decent system of laws to keep the barbarian in line, otherwise he gets away with murder. He might kill you or me and that's not on. We have our own survival instinct, thank you very much. Mind you, we are modern and while we half envy the barbarian because he has no conscience, we must insist on our various attempts to live in both worlds: the world of thoughts and the world of feelings. The world of liberty and the world of tradition. The public and the private world. And so on. The modern attempts to accomplish the impossible are potentially infinite. One gains Brownie points by joining a tribe. A tribe of scientists. A tribe of sectarians. A tribe of racists. Modern means tragic. If I cannot force my will on you I take a train to Never-never-land. There I follow the conventional lead. If I want to get something off my chest I take medication for it. The Barbarian pretends he can do without me but I know he can't. My security system is foolproof in that it fools me into supposing, most of the time, except when I wake up after a hangover, or when it occurs to me to dream about happiness, or when sex undermines my concept of social justice, that … I forgot what I was going to say.

*

The way eternal life makes itself known initially in that it draws the contradiction in every one of our blood cells to our attention. This, theoretically, is before we become modern. It draws this to our attention in a million and one ways but basically we notice that something 'is not as it was'. The philosopher might say that we are no longer ancient and have just noticed it. We add two and two and the answer turns out five. What's going on! We speak to an old friend and he turns a cold eye. Wait a minute, what's that about! We might call it a problem, but all the probing in the world yields no solution. I have to tell you, it makes me nervous. There's an enemy about somewhere. Let's band together and find him. But then the lot of us babble nonsense.

Technically we are not yet modern because we have not yet identified two opposing sides and cast our lot in with one of them, for the time being. We are still observing the apparent change. We have courage. Something must be done and any moment it will occur to us what it is.

That moment does not arrive. We become anxious. Anxiety sets in. Suddenly it's there. A fire near the heart region. We are ready to burst into a passion of tears. Instead we talk gibberish. We stare into the face of the next stranger we meet and we see that same look of total confusion in his eyes. Shall we sit down and talk it over? No, let's pretend that nothing has changed. Being able to pretend is a gift. Might as well make use of it. "Nothing to see here, folks, keep moving!" cries the policeman as the medics wheel the body out on a stretcher moments before the house bursts into flames. Now even the policeman runs for his life.

My attempt to identify the turning-point from ancient to modern is highly theoretical. What exactly *is* the point? I end up saying what I did not mean to say and then letting it stand. It shows that I'm involved. And what a good thing too – whispers my guiding spirit. As it turns out, there is no way of not being involved. After all I have no intention of coming up with a modern explanation of modernity. The libraries are bursting at the seams due to the sheer plethora of such explanations; such descriptions, justifications and whitewashes.

What interests me especially however is how those deal with the unavoidable change who have known someone who predicted it – in a variety of ways, to be sure – and then he died. Well, he was murdered, let's face it. He had predicted that too. What was most confusing was that he promised he would die and then live again. Or did he? No, it wasn't quite that simple. A hundred years later it was simplified but at the time it was not that simple. This man, this individual, this person – well, he used the language in a way that was not always clear to them – and sometimes they were downright frightened by the way he used it. He almost sounded as if he knew the world was being turned upside down and that afterwards the change would be so complete that one would not be able to speak of two versions of the same world. Like here is an apple. I am going to throw it to you now. You will try to catch it but you will have eaten it. Don't think about it, just try to catch it. And don't join the accumulating crowd of those who insist on comparing the before and the after. They will forever disagree about the before and after what, in particular. It will take you a while to get used to those new shoes. You have to wear them in. Keep at it. If the pain gets too much, lean on me.

Sorry? Lean on you? But you'll be gone!

Only in a way. Stay loose. Don't tie yourself down to absolute definitions. I cannot explain it in language you will then have to come up with for yourselves. I can only hint. Try to discover the faith you were born with and then use it to come to terms with your human nature as it will be then. That's alright, have a good cry now. Lean your head on my shoulder. Those are tears of despair and gratitude. I wish you could be as sure as I am that tomorrow everything will be different and potentially perfect. Potentially perfect. I'll be around to give you a hand. Appearance will not be as now but steeped in mercy. The earth you stand on at the moment seems hollow and you have got used to that feeling. You depend on it being hollow. I'm sorry about that. I wish it hadn't come to that. But it has, so there you have it. Afterwards it will be full. The earth will be solid. The sky will fall down and land on it and the patch you will have cultivated will burst into blooms and fruit. Here, dry your tears with this tissue. They are coming for me. They cannot help themselves. Not to worry. Honestly. You will have new eyes and you will see the new me. You will have a new stomach and you will digest the new me.

*

After he was gone we continued for a while in this mixture of hope and fear, of fear and hope. The fact that we banded together did not always seem to be the best thing to do, because these hysterical outbursts happened, which did not affect some who remained on the sidelines. They had the courage to observe what was going on within themselves. They were the ones who eventually came up with the goods. If only there had been more of them. All too often the crowd mentality insisted on itself and then of course mercy was overruled. No real mercy can flow from lawful institution. So to that extent everything went on hold. But only to that extent. The tree of life has pushed its roots deep into the soil. I know that and you know it. It's not the sort of thing you read about in the newspaper.

* *

At this stage now it seems absurd, and sad, that anyone should have a difficulty with eternal life in time. Can we not just agree that time pertains to earth and that we live on earth, which is to say upon the earth, and not immersed in it up to the waist? Mind you, the main consideration always and again persuades us of the fact that eternal life arrives within us and radiates outwards. So it makes sense that if we look to the earth for eternal life we will be frustrated.

When you see how people abuse the earth you can tell that they do in fact look for eternal life and the nature of the abuse is ever such that one might call it an impropriety. "You are looking in the wrong place!" we feel like shouting at them – as if shouting could do any good. "You knock yourselves out wanting to own pieces of the earth when you might own pieces of your human nature – at leisure." Some pretend that they are happy owning pieces of the earth and then others of course have to try to take it away from them, because they want to be happy too. What, in the end, is a nation state except a piece of the earth and a group of people insisting that they own it. If we didn't own a piece of the earth, they say, we would be lost forever. We want to live forever. Is that not the same as living eternally?

Well, no, it isn't. Forever is time, not eternal. It's a strange concept, this 'living for ever and ever'. For thine is the kingdom for ever and ever, but please rent us a piece of it – with a lease-hold agreement of ninety-nine years, if possible. You are the landlord and we doff our cap. Now please try to see things our way. What did you say? You want us to see them your way? But that means we would have to change in a whole lot of ways. I don't see that happening. We are too attached to our ways and means, as you would be after all this time. We are modern and proud of it. The modern individual looks upon himself as having arrived, there is no way of getting around that. Whatever ails him can be improved by becoming more modern. But you know something? Those who live eternally have no problem with that. All that pertains to the earth, including those who swear by the earth, is simply respected and appreciated. For them, that is the correct attitude to the earth. The elements, the weather, the storms at sea, the tortuous rock formations that testify to the crises and upheavals in the past; then the plants, the animals and the people, all of that needs to be appreciated and not criticized. And we can do it. Respect, for god's sake! People want to be told that they're doing their best. Leave them alone to get on with it. Stop interfering with the way they want to be modern. Let them be modern. Encourage them. They need to find out for themselves that happiness in the light of day cannot be achieved. Be modest, be small and your share will come to you. Gloat and it will be taken away from you – by other people, not by god. God has nothing to do with that. You bring it all on yourselves.

Since the year dot people have invented for themselves a mighty God. Why? Because they themselves want to be mighty. It stands to reason. Even in the schoolyard, I am liable to threaten the bully with my big brother – who doesn't exist. The mighty god, God, who might or might not stick up for me. The sacrificial bribe might do the trick. Look, what a good boy I've been. I live and let live. I never hurt a fly. All I want is that piece of earth-happiness. I will gladly call it something else. I will agree with a million others to call it whatever is required to get me into the club. The more of us there are, the righter we are, that makes sense, doesn't it? Everybody wants to belong. You want to be part of something bigger, don't you? We're all the same. Christ came to make us feel good.

But something is missing. All I have to do is open my mouth and I realize that things are not as they should be. Things want to be beings. People want to be human and philosophers want to be able to tie their shoelaces without getting caught up in the principle of moments. Everybody wants something. I myself am looking for a suitable end to this essay and I have to admit that after all it's not entirely up to me. I work in cooperation with merciful good spirit and my end product is always yet again another aspect of world without end, of the kingdom of heaven on earth, of reality done and dusted. It's rewarding work. I gladly let those who approach me with their critical judgment have their say. Why would I not? I wish them well.

My champion corresponds to my human-natural faith. That is where my love for all that exists on earth originates. When I go for a walk I pick off a sprig of cow parsley and crush the stem between my fingers. The pungent scent oh so immediately transports me into my childhood when I took great delight in familiarizing myself with my blooming meadow environment by way of my nose. To this day I can recall the exact marks on the wings of butterflies, on the carapace of beetles. The spider webs on the grass with their glistening dew drops and my wet bare feet. That was more than seventy years ago and then as now I couldn't believe that I was born to do other than to appreciate all that travelled under the name of creation.

When I pick a topic today – which is the same as to say: when a topic is picked for me, I know that afterwards I will not be the person I was before. Which also means that the life that comes my way will announce itself differently and I need to be ready for that. The work we do, once we have set out on the path of our resurrection, properly renders us suitable for more life. It would be wrong, I suppose, to think of eternal life as a reward, because certainly one does not have it in mind or at heart when doing it. One does not fashion one's work in line with eternal life expectations. Nonetheless the all-empowering satisfaction that is time and again seen to be building, allows itself to be called eternal life and one's time on earth is beautifully informed by it. If asked to describe it as such, one cannot. The best one can say is: neither internal nor external but eternal. Neither experienced nor felt but simply known and understood.

One sign of eternal life, I suppose, is that once one lives eternally one wants for nothing else. One's time on earth is 'para dies', to coin a word. One has conversations with one's god. These conversations are not startling or problematic but simple and straightforward. For every thought a parallel thought is available that prompts, confirms, perhaps corrects or redirects. The friend one has in god substantiates all other friendships.

At the beginning, of course, one has to build the courage of one's faith. Hopefully by then one has not sacrificed one's childhood. Or is it even possible to partake of eternal life while parts of one's previous existence still 'hang loose' as it were; while resentments and vanities still linger unresolved? I think not. I myself wrote artworks to pinpoint and recreate what was painfully-mercifully revealed to me as accumulated fixations, neuroses and psychoses, to make room and space for new life. So surely some sort of preparation like that has to come first. Why not admit right from the start, I wonder, that what one does is done for others; for a few, for several or for many. All work succeeds in that direction. All the cleansing that goes on, is that to be understood as on purpose self-centred? As self-perfection? I think not. We would be putting barriers up even as we clear the road. If and while the envisioned reward is eternal life, one cannot but behave and act ethically, in whatever direction one exerts oneself. While inward and outward are still to some degree disparate or incongruent, one is liable to worry. On occasion worry is unavoidable. Food, shelter, personal attachments all point to themselves, angrily or fearfully – in reality, if we can believe it, not to draw our attention to money or to kindness owed to family and friends but to show us what needs to be looked at hard and overcome. In a somewhat mysterious sense, reverence for ourselves is not to be distinguished from reverence for others who will set out on this path and who need all the encouragement they can get. At the same time, even while we still agonize over what we feel obliged to leave behind, miracles happen. We perceive them as miracles because they enter our life at precisely the right time, as unexpected responses to cries for help. Then we understand what it means to ask for help. We know that what will really help does not at all necessarily bear any resemblance to what we would come up with if we first thought about it. We learn how simply to lean in the direction of our god, who predicts every one of our emergencies and knows much better what would be good for us to be getting on with than we do. If we allow ourselves to think and perhaps even to speak of the will of our god, then we would do well to know him as ethical throughout and to predispose ourselves ethically.

So forget your standing as a citizen in public. That will take care of itself. And ignore the 'good man' that tries to lay claim now and again to your time and effort. You cannot *be* good. However you can *do* good. The perfect time to do good is when you have eternal life in time – when your heaven is on earth. The healthy tension between the two is a joyful call for expression. How remarkable that you cannot even *be* without making it known how, why and what you *are*. The quality and quantity of your being, even before you raise a finger, asks questions of your community that it feels obliged to answer.

This reminds us again that eternal life in time is communal. You know yourself to be in touch with all who live eternally in time. When you hear those who speak of communion with the dead in heaven call to mind that your god is not of the dead but of the living and that therefore your community includes all those for whom you do your work and who do their work also for you. It begins with your ethical attitude, your caring preoccupation, your existence for good reason. Prayer is the dynamic. Contemplation and recollection play into it. Sustained good will makes all the difference in the world. Still you have not raised a finger while you strive to be inwardly in tact, in touch with your god and physically all of a piece towards beneficial behaviour in the light of day. You do not practice mystical union in order to be able to stand before God some day as a good person but you are in touch with god here and now as you order your capacities and discipline your strengths for behaviour in the light of day. Even all this that I have mentioned so far does not go on in private or in public but in communion. This communion is entertained by you perhaps while you do your shopping or on the way to the

Lammas fair. It is the being-aspect of eternal life in time and whatever you do is informed by it. If I now describe ethical doing in comparison to ethical being, that does not mean that in reality the former has to precede the latter or that it is a necessary preparation for it. Being and doing go hand in hand. We tease the various strands of reality apart so as to be able to talk about them, to speak of them and, as in the present case, to write them down. If we have only a little of the wisdom of a child we will wish to do very little of this teasing apart, this raising of the fibres. It is the teacher's task however to create bonds and contacts and connections for those who may choose to benefit from what he has learned.

So what we may describe as ethical doing in comparison to ethical being comprises our behaviour and our actions, such as what we produce, accomplish and achieve. It streams out of us joyfully and then it comes to a halt, comes up against something that wishes to be overcome, and this we describe as being creative and recreative. Our overriding passion is to share with others the beauty and riches of our god and to demonstrate his mercy and power. "Why are we here?" we ask. "Why simply to benefit those who are not yet here." So we suffer with those who are in pain and have not yet begun to suffer. We wish those well who are caught up in grim deliberations and lend a helping hand to those who are stuck. In a crowd we do not draw attention to ourselves but in the company of a few we might speak, in case there is anyone who hears. Whatever pain we incur we suffer as quickly as possible in the understanding that all pain draws our attention to progress to be made and growth to be achieved. We are not impartial dispensers of supernatural blessings but we participate personally in time on earth so that our god may do the same. Our god is not supernatural but human-natural. If we choose to speak of 'the kingdom of god' or of 'the kingdom of heaven' we mainly wish to draw comparison to the kingdoms of the world and to emphasize the fact that a merciful authority within us wishes to show how love completes law and that it has done so.

*

Residence in the kingdom of god on earth implies first and foremost not a privilege for enjoying a state of supreme, irresponsible happiness but rather a way to work and an attitude to work that is incomparable. In fact I can think of only one reason why one should wish to live in the kingdom of god and that is the immediate proximity to god and consequently the collaboration and cooperation with god in resurrection passion and action. It is incomparable, this resurrection passion and action, because one no longer refers to one's experience or delegates one's thought and feeling processes to tradition established or otherwise but one removes oneself entirely from conflicting desires and prompts and waits for time-appropriate, contemporary truth to be revealed. Once we realize that the accent is on ethical work, there is no more need to worry about those in the modern or even the ancient past who 'were good' and did not make it into the Kingdom. The resurrection work has been available for two millennia and those who during that time were waiting for an invitation to a supernatural state were no different from those who are waiting today. Job-seekers allowance is available, but only to the extent that one actually seeks.

The secondary benefit of being and working in the kingdom of god is that one is rid of one's own hardships, which one had brought on oneself, for example by resisting evil rather than by doing good, and is privileged to be able to help others by assuming their particular hardships. Such vicarious suffering is, of course, the very warp and woof of compassionate love which, in retrospect, colours and ornaments eternal living. Once we have learned how to practice this love we no longer crave this rush of drunken glorification when the 'son of man' is to arrive on the clouds to impress his army of benevolent terrorists. The only sense the 'clouds of heaven' now make is the imagination captivated by the brain, and there I can testify to an experience or two. However when the chips are down it's each to his own soul.

As for mystical experiences, glorious visions, inebriations of beauty, divine orchestrations of human feelings and tastes – there is no shortage of those, however one does well to entertain them with a grain of salt. "Salt must be." Let each one who has arrived and is about to commence his resurrection, search within himself for his tools, for his skills and strategies. Let him not be slow to ask for advice, both for himself and for others. May he ask above all else for wisdom, for wisdom is the expertise we share with our father.

* * *

A few words about the power of believing:

Whether or not we believe, what we believe, and lastly how we believe, in other words what we mean when we say we believe something – again in other words the power of believing: is it a part of the power of thought in general? Or does believing stem, organically, from a source all its own within our human-natural being?

I intend to give a few hints here of what I myself hope to achieve, ever, by believing, by believing in.

Believing as a type of achieving – this might be a good start. I can really only believe something if a kind of guarantee for it exists within myself. This seems to be crucial, that believing cannot succeed unless what I propose to believe is ready to respond in my human nature. I create a bond, by means of my believing, between an outward something and its inward – what shall we call it – its inward body in me. Something without body acquires body through my believing it and this body it acquires is alive within me.

My body is my vision, my senses, feeling and passion. If I propose to believe something now, you might say that I extend myself bodily towards it, in the knowledge that a living link or relation with it might be possible. There is no guarantee.

I cannot believe whatever I like. By this I mean that, since something will be added on to me, it must be of use to me. It has to aid and abet my growth. And my growth has its organic time. I may succeed in believing something tomorrow but today I am not yet ready for it.

Now of course thinking also implies an appropriation of something, so I ask myself: Is believing perhaps a part of thinking? When I think something through, I consider it from several sides with the intention of acquiring whatever just then would be good for me to possess in the interest of my growth. In order for it to be of benefit to me it has to be true and if it is true, surely I automatically believe it.

So believing goes on while I think. Or lets put it this way: While I think I undertake to create connections with what will be useful for me to possess, so I have to be ready to confirm those connections if the time comes. Then, if I want to emphasize the possession-taking part of thinking, I can call it believing. What I believe I appropriate. I would neither wish nor be able to appropriate what is not true. Even at this moment, as I think about what I intend to mean by believing, I find myself repeatedly refreshing my thought-dynamic and what I keep asking is: Will this or that be more useful for me? I intend to live with what I believe, so it has to be right for me. Often I find myself coming very close to adopting some strain of thought but finally I cannot quite assimilate all of it but only some part of it and only provisionally, for the time being until I have made a few more inquiries or until I have grown more – that sort of thing.

So even at the moment I am not attempting to come up with some absolutely acceptable definition of believing – with something that you too have to accept if you are to believe – but I want to describe, for your benefit, how I at the moment understand this business of accepting something as true; of appropriating it spiritually. Let's face it, by tomorrow my insight into this bit of reality will have increased, I will see further, I will wish to emphasize some entirely new aspect of it.

It makes no sense to me to consider whether something I think and believe is right or correct unless at the same time I ask: Is it right and correct for me. This is how it has to be once we have set out upon our evolution. We waste our time by trying to find a denominator that is common to our evolution and our previous development, so we might as well make our peace with the fact that we lead exemplary lives in every sense of the word and that therefore we are responsible for our own personal creative thinking and believing. We should no more try to make others believe as we do than we ourselves intend to believe as others do. Our works reveal where we stand at the moment and they point towards where we intend to go.

I believe in the importance, for me, of merciful good spirit because it addresses me personally and I can cooperate with it. It makes good sense to me to speak of merciful good spirit as my father, because the father-son relationship is primary, to my way of thinking. It explains a great deal for me when I reflect on my growth through development into where I am now. So it suits me immensely to address merciful good spirit as my father – largely because he also addresses me as his son.

Believing, for me, is an approach. It takes time for me to believe what I believe. Believing in merciful good spirit has never let me down. On the contrary, it strengthens and empowers me. Of course I can accept something as true while I see whether or not it will work. It might work for me for the time being but then I leave it alone and concentrate on something more relevant to the moment. Those who insist on their development – which means they have stopped developing – will always try to make others believe what they themselves believe but what they mean by believing is a grasping and holding and defending against those who, they suppose, want to take it away from them. True development towards evolution has to be tentative; steering a course between seemingly opposing forces in a spirit of patience and forgiveness. What I believed as a teenager was that unless I ploughed ahead I would get stuck; that I would have to keep moving so as to discover where I was going; that I would probably be alright tomorrow if I paid close attention to what was going on today; that there was probably more to life and to me than I had a right to expect. Today I think of that as 'not really believing'. Well of course. I did not really live. I did not really exist. The developmental reality is not the evolutionary reality. While we develop we are bound to imagine our evolution in mythic fashion, as above the clouds or in the clouds and hopefully arriving on earth sometime in the future. We believe eschatologically. At the same time, if we are fortunate, we will come across the works of those who are presently evolving and we will wonder what this is about. That sense of wonder is important. Nothing that the evolving human being does – I mean his works – does not to some degree extend an invitation to developing human beings who do not insist on their development but remain open to 'what is to come'.

Developmental believing can, in itself, have nothing in common with evolutionary believing but due to that sense of wonder, especially if periodically confirmed and sustained for lengthy periods, the door is left open to the timely arrival of the evolutionary sensibility. Then that person, who is willing to entertain a change of heart and mind and not irretrievably wedded to being right, will eventually be able to believe that he is ready to evolve. What an adventure opens out for him now! At first it seems unbelievable, but that is only because he still tries to believe in the 'old' way. Eventually he will shout joyfully: I was dead and now I live! Then he may get a painful reminder that he is not here to self-indulgence but to get down to business in the interest of the living truth and its construction as endless world.

* * *

A few words about the appearance of the kingdom of god:

Those who wonder about this might benefit from what I come up with here. To start with: During his evolution, a human being is in the kingdom of god. There is no reason why the discrepancies that distinguish Jewish from Gentile thinking should prevent us from making up our mind about what is in reality the central motivation of human thought. We try to imagine what people mean when they say that the kingdom of god has not appeared yet. So we might try to explain: For the one who evolves, appearance is not the same as when he developed. What about when someone has evolved, does he …

Stop right there. When someone *has evolved* he is "like unto the angels" to borrow that phrase. Both benign and militant idiocies can develop when our development goes awry. In that case our mind draws attention to itself as under the duress of time as an influence. We develop sanely enough in time when suddenly from somewhere we get the idea that we have to hurry things along, so we whip our emotions into a sweat and let our thoughts drift in the wind. We get confused about trying to make something happen that has happened long ago and we hope to expedite matters by insisting on picturing them. How quaint when someone tries to reinvent the wheel but here we are inventing the square wheel. It won't even work.

When we allow time to influence us we behave foolishly. The image of a kingdom not as an orderly system of checks and balances but as a lofty bubble might occur to us, a bubble in which we float divested of whatever ails us. However when we rush our development we make mistakes. We lose track of the truth that development is towards evolution. Christianity must be towards the kingdom of god here and now. Compare it by all means to the way a flower develops towards the fruit and keep in mind

that fruition takes time. Imaginative and insightful contemplation of what the wonder of fruition amounts to might get us on
the right track. Now if some trickster comes along and asks you:
If an apple blossom has been fertilized three times, by a bee, a
butterfly and lastly by a hummingbird, then after fruition, which
of these three gets the credit for it? then you might simply say:
After fruition that apple falls to the ground.

Fruition takes time. Ask that apple tree. It takes both time and
the sort of knowhow that comes along with the time of fruition.
My own apple trees showed a mass of blooms this spring and
then came frost. I will maybe get five or six apples in Septem-
ber. I think something like that has happened to Christianity.
Witness, meanwhile, the struggles among the devotees to the
bee, to the butterfly and to the hummingbird.

Time is a gift of god and by abusing it we abuse ourselves. If
someone asks you when will he kingdom of god finally appear,
ask him kindly to explain himself. That may give you the oppor-
tunity to instil a bit of patience as you lead the questioner back
to the developmental path. You might introduce him to something like the four last things of the developmental period. It
won't be easy, because of the four last prejudices under which
he will probably be labouring. Anyway, if you give it time, the
spirit of truth will help you to say the right thing – or to walk
away. When feelings run high, wisdom is smart to lie low.

Whatever appears does so to become part of the world. The
stars appear. Look, there they are. Really you have no idea why
they appear. They just do. Was there a time when they did not
appear? Who can say. As for the kingdom of god, what appears
is the works of those who evolve. They are being resurrected,
they participate in the resurrection and they cooperate with
their god in the resurrection of all that needs to be resurrected.
Really there is a whole lot of that.

Will a time ever come when nothing exists that has not been
resurrected? When an apple suddenly appear in my hand fully

formed and I will throw it away because I have no appetite? Let's face it, what that question implies is: Will the time ever come when I will no longer be criticized, when I no longer have to labour in the sweat of my brow, when my enemies will be trodden underfoot, when the sun will always shine whenever I want to go for a stroll – and so on. The response to such a question perhaps ought, on occasion, to be: Look to your development. Learn wisdom. Peruse the Gospels. Be merciful. Welcome into your life the one who for the first time demonstrated the path to glory. Even a taste of eternal life in time is worth every effort you can muster. And don't let anyone persuade you that a taste is all you can have. Mostly the persuaders are those who do not even have a taste. The kingdom of god is now. Human evolution is neither a fairytale nor an extinct theory but what is in store for you if you want it.

* * * * *